ADVENT
SEASON OF PROMISE

WORSHIP THROUGH THE SEASONS

DAVID M. EDWARDS

B&H
PUBLISHING GROUP
NASHVILLE, TENNESSEE

Advent: Season of Promise
Worship Through the Seasons Series
Copyright © 2006 by David M. Edwards
All Rights Reserved

ISBN 0-8054-4324-X
ISBN 13: 978-0-8054-4324-0
Broadman & Holman Publishers
Nashville, Tennessee
www.broadmanholman.com

Dewey Decimal Classification: 242
Devotional Literature \ Worship

Printed in China
1 2 3 4 09 08 07 06

To Daniel

I will forever treasure all of our
Christmas memories growing up.

Love, David

What sweeter music can we bring
Than a carol, for to sing
The birth of this our heavenly King?
Awake the voice! Awake the string!
Dark and dull night, fly hence away,
And give the honour to this day,
That sees December turned to May.

Why does the chilling winter's morn
Smile, like a field beset with corn?
Or smell like a meadow newly-shorn,
Thus, on the sudden? Come and see
The cause, why things thus fragrant be:
'Tis He is born, whose quickening birth
Gives life and lustre, public mirth,
To heaven, and the under-earth.

We see Him come, and know Him ours
Who, with His sunshine and His showers,
Turns all the patient ground to flowers.
The darling of the world is come,
And fit it is, we find a room
To welcome Him. The nobler part
Of all the house here, is the heart.

Which we will give Him; and bequeath
This holly, and this ivy wreath,
To do Him honour; who's our King,
And Lord of all this revelling.
What sweeter music can we bring,
Than a carol, for to sing
The birth of this our heavenly King?

—Robert Herrick (1591–1674)

Season of Promise is one of four books in a devotional series called *Worship Through the Seasons*. These seasonal books mirror the calendar year: Advent, Easter, Pentecost, Harvest. Rather than using a daily devotional template, I wanted to offer writings that would coincide with a particular time of the year and could be read and contemplated throughout that season. My hope is to make the year meaningful as you discover topics and Scriptures themed for each season.

Season of Promise represents **Advent**—that fragrant season of expectation, light, music, wonder, and Christ Child. This set of writings centers around Christmas as the fulfillment of heaven's promise, embodied in a tiny baby who came to change our world forever. May these words lead you to a place of thanksgiving—a place where you can more clearly recognize that beyond the manger lies a cross and an empty tomb! Walk with me through God's *Season of Promise*.

> *The Spirit of the Lord God is on Me, because the Lord has anointed Me to bring good news to the poor. He has sent Me to heal the brokenhearted, to proclaim*

liberty to the captives, and freedom to the prisoners; to proclaim the year of the Lord's favor, and the day of our God's vengeance; to comfort all who mourn, to provide for those who mourn in Zion; to give them a crown of beauty instead of ashes, festive oil instead of mourning, and splendid clothes instead of despair. And they will be called righteous trees, planted by the Lord, to glorify Him.

Isaiah 61:1-3

CHAPTER 1

THE PROMISE OF CHRISTMAS

WORDS OF PROMISE FROM GENESIS 3:14–15

CHRISTMAS! IT'S ALMOST CHRISTMAS! Again we put up the tree, hang the ornaments, string the lights, bake the cookies, and whatever else you do at your house this time of year.

And again we tell the story—His story—because without Him there'd be no Christmas and certainly no reason for all this revelry! The very word "Christmas" is derived from the "Christ Mass," which was a celebration of God coming in the flesh to love us on a deeply personal level.

While many Christmas traditions had their origin within the last 200 years, the real Christmas started very long ago. In fact, Christmas began even before Jesus' birth some 2,000 years ago! You have to go further back than Bethlehem to find the origins of Christmas. Christmas began in the Garden of Eden, where a promise was made to a serpent—the devil—that Christmas was on its way, when God said . . .

Because you have done this,
you are cursed more than all cattle,
and more than every beast of the field;
on your belly you shall go,
and you shall eat dust
all the days of your life.
And I will put enmity
between you and the woman,
and between your seed and her Seed;
He shall bruise your head,
and you shall bruise His heel.

Genesis 3:14–15, NKJV

Thus, we have the first Christmas prophecy and promise, that at some point in history the woman would bear a Child—a second Adam—whose purpose in life would be to crush Satan's authority and power. These shades of Christmas continue to appear throughout the Old Testament: in Israel's feasts and holy days, through the voice of the prophets and the various Christophanies that appear in Scripture. Let the sheer volume of this remind you: God always keeps His promises!

Even before the Genesis account, of course, Jesus was already there. "In the beginning was the Word, and the Word was with God, and the Word was God. He was with God in the beginning" (John 1:1–2). Jesus is the eternal Son of God. Though He had a beginning on earth, there is no beginning to Him in glory. He always has been and always will be.

Jesus Christ is the same yesterday, today, and forever. No need to search for His genesis—you will not find it. There is no beginning to Him, and there will be no end. He has made everything that has ever been made, and He is still holding everything together. Every atom, every molecule—all are held together by the Son of God! (see John 1:3–10; Eph. 3:8–10; Col. 1:15–18; Heb. 11:3).

Before there was a "Silent Night," there was a silent void above the face of the deep until the Son of God began to speak the world into existence. Before "Hark! The Herald Angels Sing," they were singing the praises of the Daystar in heaven, whose light shines brighter than a million suns. Before "The First Noel," He was the first and the last, the Alpha and Omega. Before "O Come All Ye Faithful," God was being faithful to His promise by sending the eternal Son in the flesh. When God in His infinite wisdom determined that the time was right for the world to receive her King, when God's heart was broken enough from hearing the sorrowful cries of people needing a Savior, when He sensed that all of Creation was groaning for His appearing, God so loved the world that He sent His only Son, that whoever believes in Him would never perish but live forever!

And that is the promise of Christmas—God kept His promise!

WHAT EXTRAVAGANT LOVE

What extravagant love, that a King would leave His throne in glory and humble Himself in order to purchase our eternity with Him! Jesus was the fulfillment of God's promise in the Garden; He came to crush the enemy of our souls. By giving His one and only Son, God showed the world a love it had never seen.

Yet that love would be displayed altogether differently about thirty-three years later. That's because Christmas did not end in

Bethlehem. It continued on to the Cross, for Jesus came not only to live but also to die, so that we who were dead in our sins might live forever. Muhammad didn't do this, Confucius didn't do this, Buddha didn't do this. You can visit the graves of all of these people and find their remains there. But the grave of Jesus is empty because of the power of a promise kept. The promise of Christmas came to pass, and there is an empty tomb that testifies to it.

> **DOES HE SPEAK AND NOT ACT, OR PROMISE AND NOT FULFILL? (NUMBERS 23:19)**

The second Adam came to start a new race—the race of the redeemed, which would include every color, language, and people group (Rev. 7:9). To those who by faith join the ranks of the redeemed, He confers kingdom power and authority on them so that we might join Him in the crushing of Satan's rule.

THE PROMISE FULFILLED

Starting with His birth and throughout His life and ministry, we see over and over again the power of God's promise fulfilled.

The birth of Jesus Christ came about this way: After His mother Mary had been engaged to Joseph, it was discovered before they came together that she was pregnant by the Holy Spirit.

So her husband Joseph, being a righteous man, and not wanting to disgrace her publicly, decided to divorce her secretly.

But after he had considered these things, an angel of the Lord suddenly appeared to him in a dream, saying, "Joseph, son of David, don't be afraid to take Mary as your wife, because what has been conceived in her is by the Holy Spirit. She will give birth to a son, and you are to name Him Jesus, because He will save His people from their sins."

Now all this took place to fulfill what was spoken by the Lord through the prophet: See, the virgin will become pregnant and give birth to a son, and they will name Him Immanuel, which is translated "God with us."

When Joseph got up from sleeping, he did as the Lord's angel had commanded him. He married her but did not know her intimately until she gave birth to a son. And he named Him Jesus.

Matthew 1:18–25

And still, the promise kept working.

The promise of Christmas was still working twelve years later when Jesus, barely a teenager, was teaching the scholars of His day in the temple in Jerusalem. The promise of Christmas was at work in the Jordan River when Jesus was baptized by His cousin, John, when the heavens opened up and a loud voice proclaimed, "This is my beloved Son. I take delight in Him!" The promise of Christmas was working when He performed His first miracle at the wedding in Cana, where He turned the water into finest wine. The promise of Christmas was working when an afflicted woman reached out in faith through the crowds, touched the hem of His garment, and was instantly healed. The promise of Christmas was at work the day Jesus stood outside Lazarus' tomb and commanded him to come forth—and he did!

The promise of Christmas was working every time the blind could see, the deaf could hear, the lame could walk, the demonic were set free, the dead were raised, and hearts were healed! Jesus was and is the Christ of Christmas, doing what He came to do.

> **IN THESE LAST DAYS, HE HAS SPOKEN TO US BY HIS SON. (HEBREWS 1:2)**

More than the manger, Christmas is the story of "how God anointed Jesus of Nazareth with the Holy Spirit and with power, and how He went about doing good and curing all who were under the tyranny of the Devil, because God was with Him" (Acts 10:38).

Jesus came to love us unconditionally so that He could heal our condition. He came to set us free from Satan's power and the powerful sway of sin. He came to live in our hearts through faith so that He could rule and reign on the inside of every person who would call on Him and claim Him as Lord. He came to raise a standard against the enemy. He came to set the captives free. He came to give you a future and a hope.

Jesus Christ came to demonstrate that God is indeed and truly love. He came because He desired a relationship with you and me. His love for you drove Him to say "yes" to His Father's request to come to this earth. Christmas made it very clear that God's most prized possession was not heaven, not glory, not the planets, not even the earth. It was (and is) *you!* Christmas is living proof that God loved the people of this world more than any other thing.

CHRISTMAS AND CALVARY

The promise of Christmas was also present in His sacrificial death at Calvary. Without Christmas, there would not have been a Gethsemane. Without Christmas, there would not have been a crucifixion. Without Christmas, there would not have been a Calvary, for Christmas was all about Calvary—the Cross!

Jesus knew when He came that He would have to die for our sins. We needed a sinless Savior and a spotless Lamb. Any serious Christian should not ever think of the manger without thinking of the Cross, too. Truly, there is no limit to His love. It is as boundless as He is. Christmas and Calvary were boundless love on display.

Though Christmas and Calvary are vastly different images in our minds, we must remember that Jesus is both the Lion and the Lamb. Born as the King the wise men sought, He also died as the perfect sacrifice in our place. On the third day after His crucifixion, the power of the promise of Christmas brought about His resurrection! The promise that brought Him to Calvary was the same promise that led Him out of a rich man's tomb.

But Christmas didn't end there. The promise of Christmas continued as the resurrected Christ appeared to many. It continued as Jesus ascended on high to be seated at the right hand of God in power and glory. The promise of Christmas swept through an upper room on the day of Pentecost, igniting the Church that would become His visible Body on earth.

And still the promise of Christmas continues, down through the centuries, because it is unlike anything the world has seen since.

Because of Christmas, we were saved. Because of Christmas, we discovered that God loves us. Because of Christmas, we can pray to the Lord. The list goes on and on. The power of the Christmas promise affects us every second of every day. And someday the promise of Christmas will usher Jesus Christ back to earth yet again to receive His own. Because of Christmas, we will live with Him forever.

Thus, Christmas will touch our lives from now throughout all eternity!

So look beyond a one-day-of-the-year holiday. Christmas is every day! God's Christmas promise will never end—because *He* will never end! Look beyond the once-a-year gift to the Father's gift to us that can be rediscovered in new ways each day of our lives. Listen with your heart beyond the familiar carols, and hear the Song of heaven that holds it all together. How blessed and privileged we are! What joy is ours!

Jesus is truly the Alpha and the Omega. He is the quote and the end-quote. He is the "I AM." He is everything you've always heard—Wonderful, Counselor, Prince of Peace, Everlasting Father, Almighty God, Lamb of God, Good Shepherd, the Way, the

Truth, the Life, King of kings and Lord of lords, the Living Water, Messiah, Savior, and Friend. He's also everything you may *not* have discovered yet—the Bishop of our Souls, Shiloh, the Anchor Behind the Veil, the Dayspring, the Bright and Morning Star, the chief Cornerstone. He is Jesus!

Jesus is the promise of Christmas that has changed our world and our lives forever. Worship and adore Him and offer up thanksgiving to God for keeping His promise made so long ago. Thank God for Christmas!

THE LIGHT OF CHRISTMAS

WORDS OF PROMISE FROM GENESIS 1:1-4

IT'S TIME TO MAKE THAT ANNUAL TRUDGE down to the basement or up to the attic to dig through the boxes and dust and the occasional dead mouse and pull out those Christmas lights.

Although some people have been known to leave Christmas lights up all year round, for most of us the lights that adorn our tree or the eaves of our house are special because they are only displayed once a year.

Christmas lights are the first things to go on the Christmas tree. Children get excited just seeing the box of Christmas lights sitting on the living room floor in early December, because they know what's coming. When we were young, my brother and I would always ask our parents to take us for a ride in the car to "see the lights" at Christmas time. There's just something enchanting about Christmas lights. And why shouldn't there be?

I've always felt that each light on every strand is shining in honor of Him. I mean, it's His birthday, right? Instead of a cake with candles, we give Him a tree with lights. Advent is all about the coming of the Light. And all of our decorating and holiday making is really about the joy that comes as a result of His coming into our lives. Christmas lights are but an expression of appreciation for the Light we behold in Jesus.

LET THERE BE LIGHT

The first thing God ever said to this world was "Let there be light"—and there was light. What's most interesting is that the sun wasn't created until day four of Creation, yet there was light on the first day! With the exception of the light that emanated from God alone, the heavens and earth had their beginnings in total darkness.

> In the beginning God created the heavens and the earth. Now the earth was formless and empty, darkness covered the surface of the watery depths, and the Spirit of God was hovering over the surface of the

waters. Then God said, "Let there be light," and there was light. God saw that the light was good, and God separated the light from the darkness.

Genesis 1:1–4

Light is the first of our Creator's works. The earth was dark and in chaos, yet God was able to bring order out of chaos. He is God, and besides Him, there is no other. God is without peer or competitor. The sun and moon are His handiwork, not His rivals. His Word is supreme; not one thing He says goes unfulfilled. He speaks and it is done. His Word and deeds reveal His omnipotence.

God's first creative act—the giving of light—reveals His love for man, the apex of His creation. For without light, the earth would still be in utter darkness and chaos. But God loved us enough to bring order out of chaos. And He began this wonderful transformation with His first divine command: "Let there be light."

"God saw that the light was good." Notice that light, not darkness, was called "good." God is biased in favor of light. By calling the light "good," God was drawing attention to its quality and its suitability for its purpose. God is good, and His goodness is reflected in all of His works. Throughout the Scriptures, "light" is often used metaphorically for life, salvation, the commandments, and the presence of God. It is the antithesis, literally and metaphorically, of "darkness."

Thus, God extinguished the darkness and the chaos when He said, "Let there be light!" God did not need the sun, moon, or stars in order to dispel the darkness. He expelled the darkness by what He said—and by who He is! "Even the darkness is not dark to You. The night shines like the day; darkness and light are alike to You" (Ps. 139:12).

A DIFFERENT KIND OF DARKNESS

Following the Fall of man in the Garden of Eden, a progressive darkness began to cover the earth. This time the darkness was not literal but something even more dreadful: spiritual darkness. This darkness arose from error, ignorance, disobedience, willful blindness, and man's rebellion against God. This darkness is an evil system absolutely opposed to the Light. Sin had brought a dimension of darkness more powerful than the darkness before Creation, a darkness that separated man from the God who loved and created Him. This darkness kept every succeeding generation from enjoying the kind of relationship that God intended for us to have with Him. Chaos and darkness had returned—not without, but within. This time the

> **"AS LONG AS I AM IN THE WORLD, I AM THE LIGHT OF THE WORLD" (JOHN 9:5)**

darkness covered all humanity, God's most prized possession. Once again the world needed God to say, "Let there be light."

And He did!

The Light of Christmas was God's response to our darkened condition. This time, He who is the dwelling place of light, the One whose own light outshines all the suns and stars of all the galaxies, came down to earth Himself in order to shine the light of His love into every darkened heart that would receive Him. Once again the darkness was powerless to dim His light. Once again He brought order out of chaos. And once again, it was good!

In the beginning was the Word,
and the Word was with God,
and the Word was God.
He was with God in the beginning.
All things were created through Him,
and apart from Him not one thing was created
that has been created.
Life was in Him,
and that life was the light of men.
That light shines in the darkness,
yet the darkness did not overcome it.

He came to His own,
and His own people did not receive Him.
But to all who did receive Him,
He gave them the right to be children of God,
to those who believe in His name.

John 1:1–5, 11–12

The word for "overcome" that John used is from the Greek word *katalambano*, which means "to seize, to grasp, to overtake and overpower." It literally means that the darkness does not gain control of the light. Thus, the darkness of separation from God has not succeeded in overcoming the Light, which is present in the *Logos* (the Word), in the divine Christ. The darkness has not been able to vanquish the power of His light. By the very existence of this Light, the whole sphere of night is overcome and deprived of its power. The darkness can in no way, shape, or form diminish even one degree the power of the Light of the world, which is Jesus Christ our Lord—the Light of Christmas!

It was our Lord's disciple, Matthew, who wrote, "The people who live in darkness have seen a great light, and for those living in the shadowland of death, light has dawned" (Matt. 4:16). What a beautiful truth: the Light of the world has come to those who live in darkness and within the shadowland of death. Death without the Lord is truly darkness—eternal darkness. But faith in Jesus can change all of that. His Light is truly the presence of illumination. He lights up our soul. Without Jesus we are in total darkness. Therefore, it becomes our divine obligation to offer up thanksgiving, praise, and worship to Him who has set us free from this present darkness.

For you were once darkness, but now you are light in the Lord. Walk as children of light (Eph. 5:8).

He has rescued us from the domain of darkness and transferred us into the kingdom of the Son He loves, in whom we have redemption, the forgiveness of sins. He is the image of the invisible God, the firstborn over all creation (Col. 1:13–15).

But you are a chosen race, a royal priesthood, a holy nation, a people for His possession, so that you may proclaim the praises of the One who called you out of darkness into His marvelous light (1 Pet. 2:9).

I was in utter darkness before Jesus Christ came into my heart and life. Thank God that there was a Light that shined in this world so I could hear the Word of God preached to me. That Word produced faith in my heart to believe on Him as Savior and Lord—as my Light! He delivered me out of my own personal darkness as well as the darkness of this world. I must ever praise Him, because through my praise I am turning the Light on—so others can see Him.

Every believer is called to mirror His glory to this dark world. If we are looking to the Light of Christmas, then we will reflect His radiance and love to those around us. And if not—shouldn't we be? Don't you want to be reflecting His glory?

> **FOR YOU ARE ALL SONS OF LIGHT AND SONS OF THE DAY. (1 THESSALONIANS 5:5)**

The Light of Christmas should be shining in our lives every day of the year. We can help expel the darkness in others by allowing Jesus to shine through our lives. As David said, "Lord, You are my lamp; the Lord illuminates my darkness" (2 Sam. 22:29).

Embrace this Light today. His light provides illumination to your soul and to your understanding. His light provides a warmth that wraps its arms around your heart in a forever embrace. His light provides radiant beams to help you see clearly the path you must take in this life.

His light will lead you home.

You can always trust His light, for truly He is the Light of the world. So go ahead—receive Him, this Light of Christmas. "Arise, shine; for your light has come, and the glory of the Lord shines over you. For look, darkness covers the earth, and total darkness the peoples; but the Lord will shine over you, and His glory will appear over you" (Isa. 60:1–2). The *first* "Let there be light" (Gen. 1:3) was God's love and concern for mankind's physical condition. The *second* "Let there be light" (John 1:5) was God's love and concern for mankind's spiritual condition.

THE EARTH COVERED IN DARKNESS ONCE MORE

Scripture records for us one more instance of darkness covering the face of the earth. This time it was not chaotic darkness, nor was it a spiritual darkness. No, this time it was the darkness of all creation weeping as the Light of the World, the Light of Christmas, hung on a cross to give His life as a ransom for many.

> *Now it was about the sixth hour, and there was darkness over all the earth until the ninth hour. Then the sun was darkened, and the veil of the temple was torn*

in two. And when Jesus had cried out with a loud voice,
He said, "Father, into Your hands I commit My spirit."
Having said this, He breathed His last.

Luke 23:44–46, NKJV

Even in death, His light did not dim, for He was accomplishing what He had come to do: to purchase our salvation. His light was reaching out from that Cross, through ages past and forward to future generations. His light was expelling forever the darkness of sin, death, hell, and the grave. His light was the guarantee of a tomorrow. His light was the dawn of a new day. Even on the Cross He was the Bright and Morning Star.

And didn't He shine? When His blood flowed from His hands, feet, and side? As tears streamed down His face? As thorns pierced His precious brow? Didn't He shine when He said, "Father, forgive them, because they do not know what they are doing"? The Light of the World. The Daystar. The Light of Christmas. Didn't He shine?

And didn't He shine on Easter morning when He rose up from the grave? And doesn't He shine when He comes to live within each believer? Doesn't He shine with every answered prayer? Doesn't He shine with each promise that pours forth from His Word?

God has placed a Christmas Light into the darkness of this sin-sick world, and that Christmas Light is so powerful, the darkness has to yield since it has nowhere to hide. When you get out your Christmas lights, think about *the* Christmas Light who came to re-establish our broken relationship with God. Christmas lights didn't originate on a tree but on a bed of straw somewhere in Bethlehem! May His Light be in you this Christmas!

> *"I am the light of the world. Anyone who follows Me will never walk in the darkness but will have the light of life" (John 8:12).*

CHAPTER 3

THE SONG OF CHRISTMAS was introduced to the world by an angelic host of heaven in the skies over Bethlehem the night Jesus was born. The words were received and passed on by shepherds who witnessed this symphonic display.

And on and on the words to this ancient song have passed from person to person around the world for some 2,000 years.

It is a song that brings glory to God for the peace He established through the giving of His one and only Son. It is a song of hope to all people, for God has favored each person with the opportunity of salvation and everlasting life. Though taught to the world so long ago, this ancient "Song of Christmas" sustains us every day of the year, for the Lord Himself is our strength and our song.

> *In the same region, shepherds were staying out in the fields and keep-*

ing watch at night over their flock. Then an angel of the Lord stood before them, and the glory of the Lord shone around them, and they were terrified. But the angel said to them, "Don't be afraid, for look, I proclaim to you good news of great joy that will be for all the people: today a Savior, who is Messiah the Lord, was born for you in the city of David. This will be the sign for you: you will find a baby wrapped snugly in cloth and lying in a manger."

Suddenly there was a multitude of the heavenly host with the angel, praising God and saying: "Glory to God in the highest heaven, and peace on earth to people He favors!"

When the angels had left them and returned to heaven, the shepherds said to one another, "Let's go straight to Bethlehem and see what has happened, which the Lord has made known to us."

Luke 2:8–15

What a sight! All of heaven was announcing His birth. Jesus was born amid His most fundamental environment: praise! Jesus came to us wrapped in praise! The hosts of heaven were singing and worshiping His majesty as He breathed His first human breath. Immanuel—God was with us. It had finally happened—the appointed time had come—the answer to our sin problem was now among us. He had become one of us. Death was cringing, hell was shaking, and the devil had to be crying. Jesus had come just like God had said!

God kept His promise to Eve and the serpent. A Savior entered our world enveloped in the Song of Christmas!

THE COMPOSER

Can you imagine a world without song? I certainly can't. It would be dreadful, to say the least. The drone of humanity desperately needs a song to sing. A song releases creativity. A song probes our hearts with its message. A song calms our agitation and brings peace to our confusion. A song makes us happy, brings color to our world, and lifts our spirits.

No, I cannot imagine our lives without song. And thanks be to God, we will never have to, for He is the Composer of Creation! He is the Giver of Life. The Lord loves songs, singing, and music, and He has built into us that same desire to compose, sing, and make music!

Did you ever think that our humming along to a tune on the radio is a God-given trait? Or singing a song in the shower? Whether you can carry a tune or not, the fact that you even like to sing is a God-given thing. It all came from Him, the Composer. And when our lives offer back to Him the song He placed within us, we become collectively a symphony of praise and worship to our great God.

What must it sound like to Him? Can you imagine what sounds fill the halls of heaven? It is a sound that never stops, never ceases, and never ends—because *He* will never end! The adoration and praise of Almighty God will go on forever—a symphony of languages, styles, rhythms, and expressions in heartfelt worship to the King of kings and the Lord of lords. It's the Song of Christmas being returned every minute of every day!

YOU HAVE A SONG TO SING

When we receive Jesus Christ as our personal Lord and Savior, a new song is placed within our hearts. God's Holy Spirit awakens us to the melody and message of the Song of Christmas. Like shepherds on the Judean hillside, we respond with great joy because it is unlike anything we have ever heard before. Its message is one of hope, peace, and great joy—"good news!"

> JOY AND GLADNESS WILL OVERTAKE THEM, AND SORROW AND SIGHING WILL FLEE.
> (ISAIAH 35:10)

From the moment our spiritual ears hear the song, our drab world becomes alive, and for the first time we hear a melody amid the noise of humanity.

We find that we quite naturally want to sing and worship Him in ways we never dreamed possible. As we journey forward in our Christian walk, we find that the Song of Christmas sustains us in times when there are no other words to say. It wraps around us and holds us tight. It warms us from the cold. As we mature in Christ, we begin to understand the power of the song of the Lord, for it lifts us, elevates our spirits, calms our minds, and builds confidence within. His Word even dwells deeper within when sung. There is something supernatural about the song of the Lord, because it is truly something beyond ourselves—it is a song that is eternal.

God's Word is full of Scriptures that encourage and instruct us to sing to the Lord and allow the Song of Christmas to find expression in our lives:

> *The Lord is my strength and my song; He has become my salvation. This is my God, and I will praise Him (Exod. 15:2).*

> *Be filled with the Spirit: speaking to one another in psalms, hymns, and spiritual songs, singing and making music to the Lord in your heart, giving thanks always for everything to God the Father in the name of our Lord Jesus Christ (Eph. 5:18–20).*

Let the message about the Messiah dwell richly among
you, teaching and admonishing one another in all wis-
dom, and singing psalms, hymns, and spiritual songs,
with gratitude in your hearts to God (Col. 3:16).

The Psalms explode with song, singing, and music—here are a few of my favorites:

You are my hiding place;
You shall preserve me from trouble;
You shall surround me with songs of deliverance
(Ps. 32:7, NKJV).

He put a new song in my mouth,
a hymn of praise to our God.
Many will see and fear,
and put their trust in the Lord (Ps. 40:3).

Deep calls unto deep at the noise of Your waterfalls;
all Your waves and billows have gone over me.

The Lord will command His lovingkindness
in the daytime, and in the night His song shall be with
me—a prayer to the God of my life (Ps. 42:7–8, NKJV).

"Deep calls unto deep" is God calling unto that part of Him—the Holy Spirit—which He has placed inside each believer. "His song" never leaves our side—even throughout the night. Surely the Lord is not only our strength and song, but His song becomes our strength indeed! We have a song to sing! A song that changed the world—our world. It now comes from within, and we carry it with us everywhere we go. How blessed and privileged we are to have the Song of Christmas dwelling in our hearts!

> **AT NIGHT I REMEMBER MY MUSIC; I MEDITATE IN MY HEART, AND MY SPIRIT PONDERS.**
> **(PSALM 77:6)**

SHARE THE SONG

You and I have been called to share this song so others can meet the Composer as well. The song we sing is an attractive song because it sings of what the world cannot offer. The song we sing is a song of absolutes. It is fulfilling, soothing, healing. It fits into every heart that will pick up the tune.

Unlike songs about nature or even human love, though they are memorable and beautiful, the Song of Christmas transcends all of that. It is eternal, promising eternal life to all who will come and sing. It offers hope here and now and a peace beyond human comprehension.

> *But you are a chosen race, a royal priesthood, a holy nation, a people for His possession, so that you may proclaim the praises of the One who called you out of darkness into His marvelous light (1 Pet. 2:9).*

Our praise of the Lord, our singing of the song, draws others to the great Composer's message of good will, peace, and joy. People are longing to hear good news and are desperate for peace. Everyone needs to know the deep sense of lasting joy that is found only in knowing Jesus. So share the song! Sing it loud and long, because we are surrounded by people with no music in their lives. There might be noise and sound, but it's not music to live by. They may have earphones on, but they're not hearing what you're hearing. Like angels and shepherds, we must share the Song of Christmas!

DON'T STOP CREATING PRAISE

God is the rhythm of life. He is the Composer of the song we sing. His Holy Spirit within is a never-ending source of creative praise. Just as God is Creator, He put the desire to create in His supreme creation, in man. Let us never stop or tire of finding new ways to communicate the Song! Even though untold hundreds of thousands of songs have been written about the Lord, we have yet to exhaust our subject. In fact, we've only just begun.

The original melody of the "Song of Christmas" was not passed down to us, only the words. Somewhere between the angels singing it and the shepherds relaying it to townspeople, the notes were forgotten. But I suppose this was intentional on God's part so that each person could make up his or her own unique melody and offer it to the King. The Composer gave you a start; now do something with it! He gave you the first words, the first line, the first few bars; now extend and expand it. Make it your own, even as David did: "I will praise You, Lord, among the nations; I will sing about Your name" (2 Sam. 22:50).

Go ahead, sing out the Song and live out the Song. Never let the song end. Never let it die out in your heart. Never let it stop emanating from your lips. Day and night keep it going. Offer it up to Him again and again every day of the year, the eternal Song of Christmas, "Glory to God in the highest!"

CHAPTER 4

CHRISTMAS WAS OVER—and what a busy one it had been. The house had been full of people many times, present after present had been distributed to loved ones and friends, and there was a great sense of completeness that filled the heart and mind as the new year began.

"And finally," Mom thought, "I've got time to clean house and put away the decorations!" She knew it would be no easy task with three little ones running around the house and having to care for them as well. But moms know how to do the impossible. This mother worked day after day to clean house and put away the decorations. Admittedly, she had to stop from time to time to tend the children.

But one time, after coming back to the packing, she noticed something strange.

She had packed away the nativity set—you know the kind, porcelain figurines with Mary, Joseph,

Baby Jesus, three kings, two shepherds, one lamb, one donkey, and one angel. But after returning to put away the decorations, she noticed that Baby Jesus was missing from the nativity box. She knew she'd put it in there just a few minutes before. Maybe it had fallen out. No, it wasn't under the tree or under the couch.

At last she found it in the toy room—it must have fallen out and rolled across the linoleum. The mother picked up the Baby Jesus and put it back in the box, laying it on top of some other boxes for their annual trip upstairs to the attic.

A short time later, the mom returned again and noticed that Baby Jesus was once again missing. This time it wasn't in the toy room, the living room, or under the tree. Maybe one of her three little angels knew the whereabouts of Baby Jesus.

"Virginia, do you know why Baby Jesus is missing from the box with the nativity set?" Seven-year-old Virginia casually replied, "Nope!" chewing her gum and trying to pull her dolly's hair out.

"Lilly, did you take Baby Jesus?"

Six-year-old Lilly just answered, "Mother, of course not!"

Finally, there was four-year-old Michael, who was always full of surprises. "Michael," asked Mom, "do you know why Baby Jesus is missing from the nativity set box?"

Michael looked sheepish. "Well . . . uh . . . you see . . ."

Just then Mom noticed something shiny—looking just like fine porcelain—sticking out just enough to be seen from Michael's pocket. She again asked Michael, who replied, "I know where He is, but He told me not to tell!"

"Why did He tell you not to tell?" his mother asks.

With a serious face, Michael says quietly, "Because Baby Jesus doesn't want to be put away with the decorations!"

WHERE DO WE PUT JESUS?

We can put Him in a lot of places—even in the attic, packed away with the Christmas decorations. Not only did Charles Dickens encourage us to keep Christmas in our hearts every day of the year, the apostle Peter told us exactly where to put and keep Jesus:

> *But in your hearts set apart Christ as Lord. Always be prepared to give an answer to everyone who asks you to give the reason for the hope that you have. But do this with gentleness and respect.*
>
> *1 Peter 3:15, NIV*

So where are you supposed to put Jesus? "In your hearts set apart Christ as Lord." We are to put Him in our hearts and keep Him there all year long.

Notice that besides keeping Him in our hearts, we are also instructed to always be prepared to explain the difference Jesus has made in our lives. Just as God's holiness is made known among the Gentiles through His people, Israel, so Christ's holiness is made known by Christians who confess Him as Lord. The task of a holy people is to make known to the world the Holy One who called them.

Godliness (which means "God in us") always invites others to ask why we have so much hope. This is yet another reason why we need to know God's Word and His truth in order to rightly witness for Christ and lead others to Him.

> **THE ONE WHO SAYS HE REMAINS IN HIM SHOULD WALK JUST AS HE WALKED. (1 JOHN 2:6)**

We are not only to put Jesus in our hearts, but Paul tells us to put Him on! "But put on the Lord Jesus Christ, and make no plans to satisfy the fleshly desires" (Romans 13:14).

To put on the Lord Jesus means to be so united and identified with Christ that we imitate His life as our pattern for living (1 John 2:6), adopt His principles, obey His commands, and become like Him. This calls for a complete rejection of immorality and the acts of our sinful nature.

HOW DOES HE DWELL IN OUR HEARTS?

Jesus Christ dwells in (lives in, takes up residence in) our hearts through faith in Him. Let's look at what the apostle Paul wrote to the church at Ephesus concerning this:

> *I pray that He may grant you, according to the riches of His glory, to be strengthened with power through His Spirit in the inner man, and that the Messiah may dwell in your hearts through faith. I pray that you, being rooted and firmly established in love, may be able to comprehend with all the saints what is the length and width, height and depth of God's love, and to know the Messiah's love that surpasses knowledge, so you may be filled with all the fullness of God.*
>
> *Ephesians 3:16–19*

To have the "inner man" strengthened by the Holy Spirit is to have our feelings, thoughts, and purposes placed more and more under His influence and direction so that the Lord can manifest His power through us in greater measure. The purpose of this strengthening is fourfold:

1. So that Jesus' presence may be established in our hearts.
2. So that we may be rooted in a sincere love for God and others.
3. So that we may comprehend with our minds, and experience in our lives, the Lord's great love for us.
4. So that we may be filled with "all the fullness of God"—that we may reflect from our innermost being both the character and qualities that belong to the Lord Jesus Christ.

> *If you confess with your mouth, "Jesus is Lord," and believe in your heart that God raised Him from the dead, you will be saved. With the heart one believes, resulting in righteousness, and with the mouth one confesses resulting in salvation (Rom. 10:9–10).*

We put Jesus in our hearts and keep Him there through faith!

HOW DO WE KNOW HE DWELLS IN OUR HEARTS?

Once we have put Jesus in our hearts by faith, how do we know He's living there continually? Here's how: "Because you are sons, God has sent the Spirit of His Son into our hearts, crying, "Abba,

Father!" (Gal. 4:6). One of the Holy Spirit's tasks is to create within God's children a feeling of filial love that causes us to know God as our Father. The life within each of us came from Him. He is the Creator and Sustainer of life.

In this verse, the term "Abba" is Aramaic, meaning "Father." It was the word Jesus used when referring to our Heavenly Father God. The combining of the Aramaic term "Abba" with the Greek term for father (*pater*) expresses a depth of intimacy, deep emotion, earnestness, warmth, and confidence by which the Spirit causes us to cry out to God with trusting, bold assurance (see Mark 14:36; Rom. 8:15, 26–27). Remember that two sure signs of the Holy Spirit's work within us are our spontaneous cries to God as Father and our spontaneous obedience to Jesus as Lord.

> THE MIND-SET OF THE SPIRIT IS LIFE AND PEACE. (ROMANS 8:6)

"Now the One who confirms us with you in Christ, and has anointed us, is God; He has also sealed us and given us the Spirit as a down payment in our hearts" (2 Cor. 1:21–22). The Holy Spirit not only assures us of our adoption into God's family, but He Himself is a deposit or guarantee of the wonderful things God has in store for us—in this life and the next!

God's Holy Spirit within is the official seal of His ownership, marking each one of us as His own treasured possession. God places something of Himself within each of us when we receive Jesus Christ as Lord and put Him on the throne of our hearts.

And that something is His Holy Spirit!

"This hope does not disappoint, because God's love has been poured out in our hearts through the Holy Spirit who was given to us" (Rom. 5:5). As Christians, we experience God's love for us as the Holy Spirit makes us aware of it in our hearts. It is His ever-presence that assures us we are His, sustains us in our sufferings, helps us to forgive, confirms the hope of our salvation, encourages our hearts to worship, and makes His Word come alive!

The very fact that the Holy Spirit is in our hearts is evidence of how much God loves us.

GOD'S PROMISE TO US

God makes a promise to those who do not put Jesus away with the decorations, the one who loves Jesus and keeps Him in his heart. To him, to her, God responds:

> *Because he is lovingly devoted to Me,*
> *I will deliver him;*
> *I will exalt him because he knows My name.*
> *When he calls out to Me, I will answer him;*
> *I will be with him in trouble;*
> *I will rescue him and give him honor.*
> *I will satisfy him with a long life*
> *and show him My salvation.*
>
> *Psalm 91:14–16*

Here the Lord Himself addresses His faithful followers—those who keep Him in their hearts every day of their lives. Because they truly love Him, God Himself promises to come to their aid in times of trouble. The secret for receiving God's protective care is a heart that is intimately attached to the Lord in gratitude and affection. He knows who such believers are, and He will be with them in trouble, hear their prayers, and give them lives full of His divine presence and provision.

Nowhere does the Bible state that our lives—even as Christians—are without hard times and trouble. But the Lord has promised us He will be present with us and will deliver and honor those who call upon Him. His presence with us will ultimately help to tip the scales that are against us in our favor! He will see us through! For those who hope in the Lord, He will renew our strength!

Remember, there's only room for one Lord and one King in your heart! God will not share space with another. There is only room for one Baby Jesus. James 4:8 says to "purify your hearts you double-minded." The term "double-minded" means simply "God and something else." There can be no "God and something else!" There can only be God!

God promises to come near all who turn from sin, purify their hearts, and call on Him in true repentance. God's nearness will bring His presence, peace, power, and love!

PUT JESUS IN FRONT OF YOU AT ALL TIMES

"I have set the Lord always before me; because He is at my right hand I shall not be moved" (Ps. 16:8, NKJV). We should seek and cherish intimate fellowship with God above all else. The Lord's continual presence at our right hand brings His guidance, protection, joy, resurrection, and eternal pleasures.

But in order to have these we must "set the Lord always before" us! Not in the attic, not packed away with other things, not cast aside, not misplaced. The Lord is to be ever before us, always in front of us, always receiving our undivided attention, always receiving our worship, praise, full adoration, and sacrifice.

Ever before us!

After Christmas is over and you pack up the decorations for their annual trek back to the attic, basement, or garage, remember to lay One thing aside, something you will need every day of the year: Baby Jesus!

A CHRISTMAS PRAYER

Lord, today, I have set You always before me.

If You are before me, no other thing will be.

If You are before me, I will be sure of the path I am to take.

If You are before me, my vision will not be clouded by trivial things.

If You are before me, I will always be drawn heavenward.

If You are before me, I will not misplace You.

If You are before me, I will never lose sight of You.

If You are before me, I will not put You away with the decorations.

Be ever and always before me, Jesus!

Amen.

CRY HOLY

MARGARET BECKER/DAVID M. EDWARDS

Verse 1
The angels cry holy, the angels cry holy
The angels cry holy
Holy is the Lamb
The angels cry worthy, the angels cry worthy,
The angels cry worthy
Worthy is the Lamb

Chorus 1
Holy, holy, holy, Lord Almighty
Worthy, worthy, worthy, Lord Almighty
Heaven's angels fall before Your throne

Verse 2
And so we cry holy, yes we cry holy
Oh we cry holy, holy is Your name
Your people cry worthy, Your people cry worthy
Let Your people cry worthy, Worthy is Your name

Chorus 2
Mercy, mercy, mercy, Lamb of glory
Lovely, lovely, lovely, Lamb of glory
All Your children fall before Your throne

GREAT I AM
DAVID M. EDWARDS/ROBIN WELTY

Verse 1

There's no height
There's no depth
That could ever separate us
From the great I Am
No mountain so high
No river to divide us
From the great I Am
O friend so true
I long to worship You
Ancient of days
Creation's cry, from earth
And sky, we praise

Verse 2

He's the source of all light
The way, the truth, the life
He is the great I Am
He's the hope we confess
The blesser of the blessed
He is the great I Am
O friend so true
I long to worship You
Ancient of days
Creation's cry, from earth
And sky, we praise

Chorus

You are the great I Am,
And you are holy
You are the great I Am
And you are worthy
You are the great I Am
And you are holy
You are the great I Am
And you are worthy, Lord
You're worthy, Lord

HOLY

DAVID M. EDWARDS

Verse 1

Cherubim and seraphim
Fly around Your throne
And myriads of angels
Offer praise to You alone
And we have come
To lift our voice
Together we all sing

Chorus

Holy, holy
Worthy is the lamb
We cry holy, holy
Worthy is the Lamb

Verse 2

A wooden cross
Stained with blood
From God's wounded Lamb
You became our sacrifice
To save us all from sin
And we have come
To lift our voice
Together we all sing

Bridge

All blessing and power
Are Yours and Yours alone
All honor and glory
Be to You and You alone

I WILL WORSHIP YOU UNTIL
DAVID M. EDWARDS

Verse 1
On high and lofty mountains
I will praise You
Giving thanks to You in the valleys below
And at every step in between
I will sing my offering of love
Before Your throne

Chorus
I will worship You until the earth comes to an end
I will worship You until I breathe my final breath
I will worship You until all the stars collide
I will worship You until You are glorified

Verse 2
In a far and distant land
I will exalt You
Yet I will lift Your name within my home
And at every place in between
I will fall down on my knees in love
Before Your throne

2002 New Spring Publishing / Nail Prince Music (ASCAP)
Admin. by Brentwood-Benson Music Publishing, Inc. / Van Ness Press (ASCAP)

DAVID M. EDWARDS

David has been in ministry for fifteen years, and new songs of worship have been pouring out of him nearly all his life. He has worked with prolific songwriters such as Margaret Becker, Ginny Owens, Chris Eaton, Steve Hindalong, Greg Nelson, Natalie Grant, Matt Brouwer, Caleb Quaye, and John Hartley.

In 2003, he began his "Power to Worship Encounter," a popular seminar where attendees not only learn about the nuts and bolts of worship but experience God's presence as well. In 2005, he was awarded *Worship Leader* Magazine's "Best Scripture Song" Award for his song, "Create In Me," featured on his *Faithfully Yours: Psalms* project with Margaret Becker. Truly, this is only the beginning.

For more on David's music and ministry, contact: The Select Artist Group, P. O. Box 1418, LaVergne, Tennessee 37086, www.theselectartistgroup.com. Or visit www.davidmedwards.com.

Besides the three companion releases in the *Worship Through the Seasons* series, David's other books include a Psalms series—*Faithfully Yours*—as well as his signature work, *Worship 365*, and the *Holman CSB® Personal Worship Bible*, with more to come.

ACKNOWLEDGEMENTS

I wish to express my sincere appreciation to my publisher, David Shepherd, for being open to the things of God and open to me. To Ken Stephens, John Thompson, Jean Eckenrode, Jeff Godby, Lawrence Kimbrough, and the entire B&H family—my sincere thanks for all you've done for me.

To my literary agent, David Sanford, and the entire staff at Sanford Communications, Inc.—thank you so much for your guidance and perseverance. I would in particular like to thank my editor, Elizabeth Jones, for a phenomenal job and for working so quickly.

To my manager, Glenda J. McNalley, I wish to express my deep appreciation for her tireless efforts on my behalf and for her unwavering friendship.

To my beautiful wife, Susan, thank you for your love and standing by my side. *I love you!* To our wonderful blessings, Tara, Elyse, and Evan—Daddy loves you so much.

To my parents, Louis and Wanda Edwards, thank you for your "provision." To my brother, Daniel, thank you for always being a faithful friend.

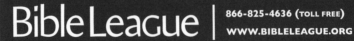

ALSO AVAILABLE FROM DAVID M. EDWARDS
AND B&H PUBLISHING GROUP

FAITHFULLY YOURS:
WORSHIPFUL DEVOTIONS FROM THE PSALMS
EACH BOOK INCLUDES A 4 SONG WORSHIP CD
CREATE IN ME ISBN: 0-8054-4329-0
ENTER HIS GATES ISBN: 0-8054-4330-4
AS HIGH AS THE HEAVENS ISBN: 0-8054-4331-2

WORSHIP 365 ISBN: 0-8054-4367-3
DAVID'S SIGNATURE WORK ON WORSHIP

THE PERSONAL WORSHIP BIBLE ISBN: 1-58640-280-3
FEATURING THE HOLMAN CHRISTIAN STANDARD BIBLE©

WORSHIP THROUGH THE SEASONS
ADVENT: SEASON OF PROMISE ISBN: 0-8054-4324-X
HARVEST: SEASON OF PROVISION ISBN: 0-8054-4333-9
EASTER: SEASON OF PASSION ISBN: 0-8054-4332-0
PENTECOST: SEASON OF POWER ISBN: 0-8054-4334-7

Available at bookstores and online retailers everywhere, or at BHPublishingGroup.com

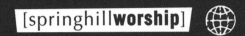